Nelson

English

Copymaster
Resource Book

1

BOOK ONE

John Jackman   Wendy Wren

Contents

Introduction

In this Copymaster Resource Book, four copymasters are supplied for use with each unit in Developing Fiction Skills Book 1 and Developing Non-fiction Skills Book 1, as follows:

- word level copymaster
- sentence level copymaster
- text level copymaster
- anthology copymaster.

The word level, sentence level and text level copymasters in this book are linked to the activities in the Pupil's Books, and may be used for support, consolidation, differentiation, extension and homework.

The anthology copymasters provide the anthology component of the course, supplementing the range of genres covered by the extended texts on which each Pupil's Book unit is based. In each unit, the stimulus material in the anthology copymaster either broadens the treatment of the unit theme but extends the range of text types, or provides an additional example of the text genre of the Pupil's Book stimulus passage. It may be used to reinforce writing activities, to provide opportunities for further text analysis and to allow pupils to revisit writing styles that have already been examined. The anthology copymasters also allow pupils to actively engage with the text, by marking and annotating the copymaster in group and class work. You can use the anthology copymasters to make overhead projector transparencies for shared text work.

Use the unit 'flag' on the side of each copymaster to help you turn quickly to the copymasters that are relevant to your current work. Fiction copymasters are marked with a black flag (unit number in white), non-fiction with a grey flag (unit number in black).

Two further copiable resources are included in this book – the **Assessment Paper** and the **Pupil Record Sheet**.

The **Assessment Paper**, designed for use at the end of the school year, will measure pupils' attainment in text level work – Reading Comprehension and Writing – and in Spelling. This Assessment is in addition to the separate Check-ups – the informal assessment tests that appear at the end of each Pupil's Book, and which focus specifically on word and sentence level work.

Depending on how you choose to administer the Assessment, it can give pupils experience of sitting a more formal test, as it is modelled on the statutory end-of-Key-Stage tests used in England. In order to simulate the booklet-style presentation of the official tests, it is recommended that you staple together the pages of the various components of the Assessment before handing them out to the children. Thus, you will create:

- A 13-page Reading Comprehension booklet (If you wish your pupils to take the Fiction and Non-fiction parts of the Reading Comprehension test at separate sittings, you will need to make two copies of the first sheet, with its instructions and space for the pupils to write their name and the date. Attach one copy to the front of the Fiction paper and one to the front of the Non-fiction paper.)
- A two-page Fiction Writing Test, comprising a sheet with story starting points, and a planning sheet.
- A two-page Non-fiction Writing Test, comprising a sheet outlining the writing task, and a planning sheet.

The Spelling test comprises a teacher's sheet for dictation, and a single pupil's sheet for their answers.

Whilst a marking scheme has not been provided for the Assessment paper, score boxes have been inserted down the right-hand side of each sheet that the children are required to fill in and on which they will be marked. This will assist you in devising your own marking scheme for the assessment, and will also help children to get used to a page layout of this kind. Please note that the planning sheets for the writing tasks are not normally marked, and these do not, therefore, include score boxes.

Timing of the Assessment Paper is not specified, but you may wish to make each component a timed paper, as appropriate to the ability of the children in your class and to simulate the conditions of a more formal test.

Answers to the Assessment paper are provided in the Teacher's Guide.

The **Pupil Record Sheet** is designed for the recording of individual pupil's progress throughout each year as they work through the units in the two Pupil's Books. You may like to make more than one photocopy of the Record Sheet for each pupil, giving children their own copies to complete as they work through the activities. Keeping a record of their achievements in this way can provide pupils with an incentive for making progress. You may also choose to use your own copy of each child's Record Sheet as the front cover of a storage folder for that child's work. This will enable you to keep together selected samples of work and the sheets of paper on which the Assessment Papers and Check-ups were undertaken, and will conveniently provide you with the necessary profiling evidence required to document each child's progress.

Synonyms

A   Draw a line to join each underlined word to its synonym. The first one has been done to help you.

1   a <u>dull</u> book   unwell

2   his <u>big</u> eyes   dad

3   her <u>sick</u> brother   sad

4   my <u>father</u>   wealthy

5   a <u>rich</u> woman   large

6   her <u>miserable</u> face   boring

B   Choose a word from the box that means almost the same as the underlined word or phrase in each sentence.

saw	truck	enjoyed	road	leaving	sad

1   William looked down the <u>street</u>.   _____

2   He noticed the removal <u>van</u>.   _____

3   William <u>watched</u> the men unload the van.   _____

4   He was <u>upset</u> about <u>moving out of</u> his room.   _____ _____

5   William <u>liked</u> playing with his train set.   _____

Verbs

Label each part of the picture with a word from the box below.

climbing

| sleeping | washing | eating | cooking | reading |
| watching | climbing ✓ | crying | sweeping | |

name _____   date _____

Your den

The walls   What are they made of? _____

Write some words you could use to describe the walls of your den:

_____   _____   _____

_____   _____   _____

_____   _____   _____

_____   _____   _____

The roof   What is it made of? _____

Write some words you could use to describe the roof of your den:

_____   _____   _____

_____   _____   _____

_____   _____   _____

_____   _____   _____

The door   What is it made of? _____

Write some words you could use to describe the door of your den:

_____   _____   _____

_____   _____   _____

_____   _____   _____

_____   _____   _____

Write some words you could use to describe how you feel when you are inside your den:

_____   _____   _____

_____   _____   _____

name _____   date _____

Brother Trouble

I'm the youngest in our house so it goes
like this:
My brother comes in and says:
'Tell him to clear the fluff
out from under his bed.'
Mum says,
'Clear the fluff
out from under your bed.'
Father says,
'You heard what your mother said.'
'What?' I say.
'The fluff,' he says.
'Clear the fluff
out from under your bed.'
So I say,
'There's fluff under his bed, too,
you know.'

So father says,
'But we're talking about the fluff
under *your* bed.'
'You will clear it up
won't you?' mum says.
So now my brother – all puffed up –
says,
'Clear the fluff
out from under your bed,
clear the fluff
out from under your bed.'
Now I'm angry. I am angry.
So I say – what shall I say?
I say,
'Shuttup Stinks
YOU CAN'T RULE MY LIFE.'

by Michael Rosen

Alphabetical order

A Fill in the missing letters.

__ b __ d __ f g __ __ j __ l __

n __ p __ __ s t __ v w __ y __

B For each letter below, write down the letter that comes next in the alphabet.

1 a __   2 f __   3 q __   4 d __

5 x __   6 b __   7 m __   8 o __

C For each letter below, write down the letter that comes before it in the alphabet.

1 __ c   2 __ j   3 __ s   4 __ z

5 __ g   6 __ l   7 __ r   8 __ b

D 1 Draw a circle around the first letter of each of these animal names.

ant   bee   cat   dog   elephant

2 What do you notice about the letters you ringed in question 1?

_____

_____

_____

What is a sentence?

A Copy these sentences, putting in the capital letters and full stops.

1 we went to visit our friends

_____

2 their house is at the seaside

_____

3 we played on the beach all day

_____

B Write three sentences about the picture. Don't forget the capital letters and full stops!

1 _____

_____

2 _____

_____

3 _____

_____

Facts about your family

How many people are in your family? _____

The names and ages of your brothers, if you have any: _____

_____

_____

The names and ages of your sisters, if you have any: _____

_____

_____

Do you have a mum? If so, what is she like? _____

_____

_____

Do you have a dad? If so, what is he like? _____

_____

_____

Who else lives with you? _____

_____

_____

What does your family enjoy doing? _____

_____

_____

On the back of this sheet, write about your family. Begin: In my family…

Different types of home

semi-detached houses

A **semi-detached house** is one that is joined on one side to another house. This type of house usually has two or three storeys (floors).

Terraced houses are rows of houses which are joined together on both sides. The house on the end of a terrace is only joined on one side. Terraced houses usually have two or three storeys.

terraced houses

detached house

A **detached house** is not attached to any other house. Detached houses usually have two or three storeys.

A **bungalow** is a one-storey house. All the rooms are on one floor, called the ground floor. A bungalow is usually detached.

bungalow

block of flats

Some buildings are divided into a number of homes, called **flats**. Most flats have just one storey. They are often built one on top of another, in a block. The flat or flats on the bottom floor are called ground-floor flats.

Name	Description	Storeys
semi-detached	joined on one side	usually two or three
terraced	joined on both sides end of terrace joined on one side	usually two or three
detached	not joined to other houses	usually two or three
bungalow	not usually joined to other houses	one
flat	in a building with one or more other flats, usually built one on top of another	usually one

unit 2

Prefix 'un'

A Write a word with the prefix 'un' that means the same as each pair of words below. The first one has been done to help you.

1 not fair   _____unfair_____   **2** not lucky   _____

3 not able   _____   **4** not true   _____

5 not known   _____   **6** not attractive _____

7 not certain   _____   **8** not conscious   _____

9 not healthy   _____   **10** not wanted   _____

B Complete each sentence with an 'un' word. The picture clues will help you.

Bob is _____ .

Your room is _____ .

The boy is _____ .

The ground is _____ .

Sentences – questions

A　Add a full stop or a question mark at the end of each sentence.

1　Where did Hansel and Gretel live _

2　Their father was a woodcutter_

3　Was the family rich or poor_

4　What was left for the family to eat _

5　There was nothing left to sell _

6　The woodcutter decided to leave the children in the forest _

7　Did he think the children would be rescued _

B　Write a word in the gap to complete each question. Add the missing question marks.

Question	Answer
1 _____ are Hansel and Gretel_	in the forest
2 _____ is Hansel cuddling his little sister_	She is afraid.
3 _____ are they both so frightened_	They don't like the dark forest.
4 _____ will they do_	try to find their way home

Setting out a playscript

Read this picture story.

Finish writing the story as a playscript. Start in the space below, and continue on the back of this sheet.

Characters:	What they say and do:
Leo	(Gloomily) I think we're lost, Raj.
Raj	_____
_____	_____
_____	_____
_____	_____
_____	_____

Nelson

English

Anthology Copymaster 2

Book 1: Fiction

name _____ date _____

unit
2

JACK AND THE BEANSTALK

Here is the beginning of a poem by Roald Dahl.

Jack's mother said, 'We're stony broke!

'Go out and find some wealthy bloke

'Who'll buy our cow. Just say she's sound

'And worth at least a hundred pound.

'But don't you dare to let him know

'That she's as old as billy-o.'

Jack led the old brown cow away,

And came back later in the day,

And said, 'Oh mumsie dear, guess what

'Your clever little boy has got.

'I got, I really don't know how,

'A super trade-in for our cow.'

The mother said, 'You little creep,

'I'll bet you sold her much too cheap.'

When Jack produced one lousy bean,

His startled mother, turning green,

Leaped high up in the air and cried,

'I'm *absolutely stupefied*!

'You crazy boy! D'you really mean

'You sold our Daisy for a bean?'

She snatched the bean. She yelled, 'You chump!'

And flung it on the rubbish-dump.

Then summoning up all her power,

She beat the boy for half an hour,

Using (and nothing could be meaner)

The handle of a vacuum-cleaner.

by Roald Dahl

'Jack and the Beanstalk' from *Revolting Rhymes* by Roald Dahl, 1982, is reproduced by kind permission of the publishers, Jonathan Cape Ltd.

unit 2

Alphabetical order

A Fill in the missing letters.

A	B	_	D	E	_	G	_	_	J	K	_	_
_	O	P	_	R	_	_	U	_	W	_	Y	Z

_	b	_	d	_	_	g	_	i	j	k	_	_
n	o	_	q	_	s	_	u	_	_	x	_	_

B Write each group of letters in alphabetical order.

1 b   c   a   __ __ __

2 Z   C   D   __ __ __

3 Q   L   B   S   __ __ __ __

4 a   s   g   k   __ __ __ __

5 Y   H   I   L   N   S   __ __ __ __ __ __

6 p   w   m   f   v   g   __ __ __ __ __ __

C Write each group of words in alphabetical order.

1 girl   boy   woman   _____

2 pen   table   computer   _____

3 hoop   ball   rope   _____

4 picture   scissors   brush   _____

5 stable   horse   jump   bucket   fence

_____

6 goal   boots   football   crowd   team

Published by Thomas Nelson and Sons Ltd   Nelson English © John Jackman and Wendy Wren 2000

Proper nouns

A Find all the proper nouns in the box. Write them down, putting in the capital letters.

march	friday	chair
hannah	teacher	
matthew	house	rabbit
mr jones	nadim	ball
february	portsmouth	
cardiff	town	sarah

_____   _____

_____   _____

_____   _____

_____   _____

_____   _____

B Copy these sentences, putting in the capital letters.

1 shaun and liam live in liverpool, but rachel lives in leeds.

_____

2 in december, we went to australia to stay with daniel over christmas.

_____

3 kate french and saiqa mohammed are in miss smith's class.

_____

4 lisa, karl and simon are coming to my party on saturday.

_____

unit 2

Key words

These key words are from a book about J M Barrie, who wrote *Peter Pan*.
Use each set of key words to write a sentence about J M Barrie.

1

| born 1860   died 1937 |

_____

2

| born Scotland |

_____

3

| father – David   mother – Margaret |

_____

_____

4

| father a weaver |

_____

5

| 1883–1890 journalist in Nottingham then London |

_____

_____

6

| Peter Pan, play, first performed 1904 |

_____

Published by Thomas Nelson and Sons Ltd   Nelson English © John Jackman and Wendy Wren 2000

Nelson

English

Anthology Copymaster 2

Book 1: Non-fiction

name _____   date _____

unit
2

Fairy stories

Fairy stories are simple tales for children. They usually involve some sort of magic, and most fairy stories have a happy ending. The wicked characters are punished and the good characters live happily ever after.

Most fairy stories are very old. At first, they would not have been written down but passed on verbally – with parents telling fairy stories to their children who, in turn, grew up and told them to their children. Writers like the Grimm brothers in Germany collected fairy stories and printed them in books, for people to read to their children.

Hans Christian Andersen did not collect other people's stories but wrote his own fairy stories. 'The Emperor's New Clothes' is one of Hans Christian Andersen's stories. Here is the beginning of the story:

The Emperor's New Clothes

Many years ago there lived an Emperor. He was very fond of fine, new clothes and spent a great deal of money on new outfits. He was always dressing up and had no time for anything else.

One day, two strangers arrived in the Emperor's palace. They asked to see the Emperor and told him they were weavers. They said they had come to make the Emperor the most beautiful new suit, but they warned him that the cloth had magical powers. Anyone who was stupid would not be able to see it.

The weavers pretended to hold out a length of the beautiful cloth but, really, there was nothing there. The Emperor did not want to be thought stupid, so he agreed it was very beautiful and the weavers set to work making his suit.

'i-e' and 'igh' letter patterns

A Write a word that rhymes with each word below and has the 'i-e' or 'igh' letter pattern. The picture clues will help you.

unit 3

1 five _____

2 line _____

3 wide _____

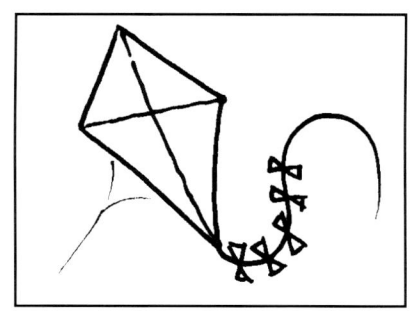

4 might _____

5 price _____

6 bite _____

7 sight _____

8 file _____

9 glide _____

B **1** Write four more words that have the 'igh' letter pattern (like 'sight').

_____ _____ _____ _____

2 Write four more words that have the 'i-e' letter pattern (like 'five').

_____ _____ _____ _____

Speech marks

Write in the speech bubbles the words you think the people are saying.

Describing settings

unit **3**

1 Colour the picture.
2 Below, write some words to describe each item.

the table: **the sink:**   **the curtains:**   **the cupboards:**

_____   _____   _____   _____

_____   _____   _____   _____

_____   _____   _____   _____

the flowers: **the floor:**   **the whole room:**

_____   _____   _____   _____

_____   _____   _____   _____

_____   _____   _____   _____

Happy Mouseday

Pete wanted a pet mouse. Every Saturday was Mouseday. After breakfast, he would ask his mum and dad if he could have a mouse. Every Saturday, his mum and dad would say no, that he could not keep a mouse in the house, so he would climb up into his tree-house to think …

The tree-house was no beauty. Pete's father had made it out of odds and ends of timber and put a tin roof on it. He had fixed it in a fork of the old apple tree. It wasn't very big, but it had a door of sorts, and a kind of window. Inside there was an old folding garden-chair for sitting on, and a shelf for keeping things on, and the whole tree-house was rainproof.

Most importantly, it was Pete's, and on its side was written in big black letters:

On this particular Mouseday, Pete was thinking about the actual words his mum or dad always used. "You are not keeping a mouse in this house," was what they said.

Suddenly he jumped up from his chair. Through the branches, he peered out across the lawn.

"OK, so I can't keep a mouse in *that* house," he said excitedly, "But what about in *this* house?"

From *Happy Mouseday* by Dick King Smith

Published by Thomas Nelson and Sons Ltd

Nelson English © John Jackman and Wendy Wren 2000

Alphabetical order

a	b	c	d	e	f	g	h	i	j	k	l	m
n	o	p	q	r	s	t	u	v	w	x	y	z

A Write each group of words in alphabetical order.

1 knife   fork   spoon

_____

2 banana   apple   cherry

_____

3 monkey   camel   elephant   anteater

_____

4 Tuesday   Monday   Saturday   Friday

_____

B Write each group of words in alphabetical order. You will need to look at the second letter of each word.

1 dark   dig   dog   deer

_____

2 rabbit   red   rocks   run

_____

3 wild   weeds   water   woods

_____

4 Andrew   Ali   Aaron   Aziz   Arthur

_____

5 Suzanne   Sonia   Sita   Shelley   Samantha

_____

Speech marks

A Use speech marks to write down what was said in this cartoon strip. The first part has been done to help you.

unit
3

1   **MUM:**   "We need some milk, Helen."

    HELEN: _____

2   **MUM:** _____

3   **HELEN:** _____

    BEN: _____

B Write down the exact words that were spoken in each sentence. The first one has been done to help you.

1   "May I go round to Lauren's house?" asked Katie.

    May I go round to Lauren's house?

2   "Yes, but ask your big sister to walk with you," Mum replied.

    _____

3   "OK," said Katie. "I'll go and ask her now."

    _____

4   "Sophie, will you walk to Lauren's with me?" Katie asked.

    _____

5   "Yes," replied Sophie, "but let's go before it rains."

    _____

name _____   date _____

Writing reports

unit 3

What animal are you writing about? _____

Write some notes about:

where it lives/sleeps: _____
_____

what it eats: _____
_____

how to look after it: _____
_____

different breeds: _____
_____

Now use your notes to write a report about the animal you have chosen.

_____
_____
_____
_____
_____
_____
_____
_____
_____
_____

Bees

Three kinds of bees live in a bee hive.
Most of the bees are small worker bees.
A few are a little bigger.
These are the male bees, called drones.

The biggest bee is the queen.
The queen stays in the hive.
She does not go out to find food.
The other bees feed her and she lays eggs.

Inside the hive is a honeycomb.
The queen lays an egg in each empty cell of the honeycomb.
After three days the eggs hatch.
At first they are grubs, then larvae, then bees

4

INDEX

	Page
cells	4, 8, 11, 12, 13, 14, 15, 17
drones	4, 5, 6
eggs	4, 7, 8, 10, 15
hive	4, 5, 6, 7, 14, 17
honeycomb	4, 8
larvae	4, 9, 10, 11, 12, 16
queen	4, 5, 6, 7, 8, 15, 16, 17, 18
worker bees	4, 7, 9, 10, 11, 15, 16, 18

'ow' letter pattern

A Complete the 'ow' word that goes with each clue.

1 a light fall of rain   sh_____

2 a large group of people   cr_____

3 to plant a seed   s_____

4 the antonym of 'high'   l_____

5 you might pick a bunch of these   f_____

6 soup is served in one of these   b_____

7 what you do with oars to make a small boat move r_____

8 what do you do to fill a balloon with air   b_____

B Sort the words from the box into two lists, depending on the sound the 'ow' letter pattern makes.

_____   _____

_____   _____

_____   _____

_____   _____

_____   _____

_____   _____

_____   _____

vowel	grow
mow	vow
throw	power
glow	flow
tower	howl
lower	fowl
growl	town

Compound nouns

A Draw a line to join each pair of words that can be put together to make a compound noun. Write out the words you have made. The first one has been done to help you.

lady	ball	ladybird
butter	bow	_____
foot	brush	_____
gold	case	_____
rain	bird	_____
hand	cup	_____
tooth	fish	_____
book	bag	_____

unit
4

B Use the picture clues to write down six compound nouns.

1  +  =

2  + ☕ =

3 🌳 + 🪥 =

4  +  = _____

5  + 🌊 =

6  + 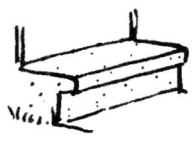 = _____

unit
4

Writing poetry

What type of animal are you writing about? _____

Draw your animal here.

Write down some words you could use to show what you like about
this type of animal.

Write down some words you could use to show what you do not like about
this type of animal.

The Laughing Snowman

unit
4

"We'll have snow before long," said Dad, looking up at the sky.

"Snow," said Mum, and she shivered.

"Snow," said Emma's sister Mandy. "Well, I won't go out. I'll stay indoors by the fire."

"Snow!" said Emma. "We haven't had snow for years!"

All day at school, she kept looking out of the window, watching for the first snowflakes. It got colder and colder, but still it didn't snow.

That night when she snuggled down under the duvet, Emma meant to stay awake – just in case it snowed during the night. But in ten minutes she was fast asleep.

When she woke up next morning, she knew right away that something had happened. There was a strange silence. Usually she could hear the rumble of traffic in the distance. Often there was a sound of a car engine spluttering into life across the way. But this morning it was very quiet.

Emma jumped out of bed and flung open the curtains.

All over the garden was a soft downy covering of pure white. Snow hung like icing sugar along the branches of the tree by the gate.

She ran through to wake up Mum and Dad. "It's snowed! Get up! Look!"

"Mmm . . ." said Dad.

"Uh-huh," said Mum.

They didn't seem a bit interested. So she went to tell Mandy.

"Go away," Mandy mumbled sleepily. "It's Saturday."

From *The Laughing Snowman* by Anne Forsythe

'ea' letter pattern

The 'ea' letter pattern sometimes makes the same sound as the 'ee' letter pattern.
For example:

Please f<u>ee</u>d the dog.   Can you r<u>ea</u>d this?

unit 4

A Choose whether to use 'ea' or 'ee' to complete each word below.

1 s w __ __ t s

2 p __ __ s

3 c o f f __ __

4 p __ __ c h

5 b __ __ f b u r g e r

6 i c e c r __ __ m

B Complete each 'ea' or 'ee' word and draw a line to match it with the correct meaning.
The first one has been done to help you.

1 f <u>e e</u> t   grows on a tree

2 wh __ __ ls   you might do this while you are asleep

3 l __ __ f   socks keep them warm

4 s __ __   a woolly animal

5 sh __ __ p   there are two on a bicycle

6 dr __ __ m   ships sail on this

Ending sentences

Copy these sentences, putting in the capital letters, full stops and question marks.

1 laura warts to go to the cinema tonight

_____

2 can we go if we promise to be back in time for tea

_____

3 we can take a bus to brighton

_____

4 we'll have to walk to hove to catch it

_____

5 what time does it leave

_____

6 on mondays and thursdays, buses leave every half hour

_____

7 wear a coat, it's cold outside

_____

8 shall i take an umbrella

_____

name _____ date _____

Contents pages

What sport have you chosen? _____

Here is my contents page:

```
                        CONTENTS
                                                        page

1  _____    _____

2  _____    _____

3  _____    _____

4  _____    _____

5  _____    _____

6  _____    _____

7  _____    _____

8  _____    _____

9  _____    _____
```

Think of a title for your book: _____

unit 4

Snow

People have different opinions about snow. Some people like it because it makes everything look pretty, and it is fun to play in the snow. Other people see snow as dangerous and a nuisance.

How snow forms

Snow is made when the air is very cold. In the clouds, water freezes and delicate crystals of ice form. Each crystal 'grows' in a repeating pattern. As the crystals touch each other, they stick together and form snowflakes. Every single snowflake is different from all the others.

The dangers of snow

Snow settles on trees and can sometimes break off branches with its weight. Farm animals can be trapped in the snow and it is hard for wild animals to find food. On the roads, snow can bring danger for people who are driving or who become stranded. In the mountains, masses of snow can crash down from higher up the mountain, burying towns and villages further down. This is known as an avalanche.

Snow sports

As well as being dangerous, snow can be fun. There are some sports that can only be done on snow, such as skiing, snowboarding and tobogganing. People who enjoy these exciting snow sports are happy when there has been a good fall of snow.

The alphabet

a	b	c	d	e	f	g	h	i	j	k	l	m
n	o	p	q	r	s	t	u	v	w	x	y	z

A Write the letter from each pair that comes first in the alphabet. Your answers should spell out a message.

unit
5

j   i   z   p   o   b   n   e

h   m   p   r   w   a   q   d

___ ___ ___ ___ ___   ___ ___ ___

f   l   e   t   j   a   v   t   a   l   y   a   z   t

e   s   y   p   h   c   n   x   b   n   w   u   y   s

___ ___ ___ ___ ___ ___ ___ ___   ___ ___ ___ ___ ___ ___

p   r   g   w   e   k

a   t   j   u   g   d

___ ___ ___ ___ ___ ___

B Here is a message in code. Use the code breaker to work out the message.

Code breaker:

A	B	C	D	E	F	G	H	I	J	K	L	M
1	2	3	4	5	6	7	8	9	10	11	12	13

N	O	P	Q	R	S	T	U	V	W	X	Y	Z
14	15	16	17	18	19	20	21	22	23	24	25	26

20   8   5   15   20   8   5   18   3   18   1   2

___ ___ ___   ___ ___ ___ ___ ___   ___ ___ ___ ___

23   1   14   20   5   4   20   15   2   5

___ ___ ___ ___ ___ ___   ___ ___   ___ ___

2   5   1   21   20   9   6   21   12   20   15   15

___ ___ ___ ___ ___ ___ ___ ___ ___   ___ ___ ___

Ending sentences

A Put a full stop (.), a question mark (?) or an exclamation mark (!) at the end of each sentence.

1 Goldfish should be kept in large tanks full of clean water __

2 Is this tank large enough __

3 Don't you dare drop that tank __

4 How many fish are there __

5 You must feed the fish every day __

B Copy each sentence, putting in the missing capital letters and punctuation marks.

1 what do you give your fish to eat

_____

2 my goldfish is called fred

_____

3 will it bite my finger

_____

4 don't be so silly

_____

5 i will ask if i can have a goldfish

_____

unit 5

Story beginnings

> You are going to write the beginning of a story about an animal that is kind to an old lady who is really a fairy. You could begin your story in three ways:
>
> **1** by describing the setting   **2** by describing the characters   **3** with a conversation

1 Describing the setting

One day, an old lady was walking along a country lane.

Write some sentences to describe the country lane.

_____

_____

_____

_____

2 Describing the characters

Once, there was a very old lady.

Write some more sentences to describe the old lady.

_____

_____

_____

_____

3 A conversation

"Good morning," said the frog to the old lady.

Write some more sentences to show what the frog and the old lady talked about.

_____

_____

_____

_____

If You Want To See An Alligator

If you want to see an alligator
you must go down to the muddy slushy
end of the old Caroony River

I know an alligator
who's living down there –
She's a-Mean. She's a-Big. She's a-Wicked
She's a-Fierce.

Yes, if you really want to see
an alligator, you must go down to the
muddy slushy end of the old Caroony River

Go down gently to that River and say.
'Alligator Mama
Alligator Mama
Alligator Mamaaaaaaaaaaaaa'

And up she'll rise
But don't stick around
RUN FOR YOUR LIFE!

by Grace Nichols

unit
5

Nelson English

Word Level Copymaster 5   Book 1: Non-fiction

name _____ date _____

Using a dictionary

Use your dictionary to help you choose the best definition for each word. Draw a line between each word and the correct definition.

A 1 **annoy**
- a type of glue
- to make someone cross
- to be very sorry

2 **fable**
- a short story with a meaning
- weak
- a book

3 **famine**
- another word for 'woman'
- a great shortage of food
- famous

4 **obedient**
- to be naughty
- a monster
- willing to obey

5 **odour**
- outside a building
- the odd-one-out
- a smell

6 **boisterous**
- lively and noisy
- a group of boys
- a type of pillow

B Use each word from part A in a sentence of your own.

1 _____

2 _____

3 _____

4 _____

5 _____

6 _____

Adjectives

A   Underline all the adjectives in this passage.

The hot sun shone out of a clear, blue sky. We played on the soft, yellow sand while our lazy Dad went to sleep under the big green umbrella. When he woke up, black clouds had appeared, big, cold raindrops were falling and the tide had come in. Poor Dad had a terrible shock!

unit
5

B   1   Colour the pictures above. Remember to match the description in part A.

2   Write three more sentences to describe the pictures.

_____

_____

_____

For and against

What subject are you writing about? _____

Write some points for and against.

For	Against
_____	_____
_____	_____
_____	_____
_____	_____
_____	_____
_____	_____
_____	_____
_____	_____
_____	_____
_____	_____

Which is your best reason for being 'for' this thing?

_____

_____

Which is your best reason for being 'against' this thing?

_____

Tigers

Tigers belong to the cat family.

Appearance

The male tiger is bigger than the female tiger. Most tigers have orangey-brown fur with black markings. These markings help them to hide in the shadows among plants and trees. There is one rare type of tiger that lives in snowy areas and has white fur, which helps it to hide in the snow.

unit
5

Habitat

Most tigers live in hot climates, such as the jungles of India. A few can be found in the cold, snowy regions of Siberia. Here, their fur is very thick to keep them warm.

Behaviour

Tigers do not live in herds or packs like some animals, but hunt on their own. They rest during the day and hunt at night. They like to catch deer and wild pigs, but they will eat almost any animal they can catch. Tigers cannot run very fast, so they have to creep very close to their prey and then pounce.

Antonyms

A Choose from the box the correct word to fill each gap.

small	dry	in	fast	thin
over	cold	closed	dirty	

1 open and _____

2 hot and _____

3 big and _____

4 _____ and out

5 _____ and under

6 _____ and slow

7 clean and _____

8 fat and _____

9 wet and _____

B Use the prefix 'un' or 'dis' to make the antonym of each word.

1 friendly _____

2 approve _____

3 believe _____

4 appear _____

5 worthy _____

6 expected _____

unit **6**

name ______________________ date ______________________

Adjectives

A In the frame below, draw or stick a picture of a famous person, a friend or someone in your family.

Make a list of at least seven adjectives to describe the person.

B Write four sentences about the person. Use as many adjectives as you can.

unit 6

Planning the plot of a story

Story title: _____

unit 6

How does your story begin?

_____

_____

_____

_____

_____

What happens in the middle of your story?

_____

_____

_____

_____

_____

How does your story end?

_____

_____

_____

_____

_____

The Witch's Brew

Into my pot there now must go
Leg of lamb and green frog's toe.

Old men's socks and dirty jeans.
A rotten egg and cold baked beans.

Hubble bubble at the double
Cooking pot stir up some trouble.

One dead fly and wild wasp's sting,
The eye of a sheep and the heart of a king.

A stolen jewel and mouldy salt.
And for good flavour a jar of malt.
Hubble bubble at the double

Cooking pot stir up some trouble.
Wing of bird and head of mouse,
Screams and howls from a haunted house.

And don't forget the pint of blood,
Or the sardine tin and clod of mud.

Hubble bubble at the double
Cooking pot stir up some TROUBLE!

by Wes Magee

The Witch's Brew by Wes Magee is reproduced by kind permission of the author.

unit
6

Contractions

A Write a contraction for each pair of words.

1 he is	**2** that is	**3** we are	**4** they are
_____	_____	_____	_____
5 you will	**6** are not	**7** he would	**8** she has
_____	_____	_____	_____
9 is not	**10** I have	**11** has not	**12** it will
_____	_____	_____	_____

B Write the pair of words from which each of these contractions has been made.

1 weren't	**2** you're	**3** I'm
_____ _____	_____ _____	_____ _____
4 wouldn't	**5** they'll	**6** you'd
_____ _____	_____ _____	_____ _____

C Copy these sentences, using contractions to replace the underlined words.

1 Winston and Ravi <u>had not</u> seen the video.

_____

2 <u>It is</u> sad when we have to say goodbye.

_____

3 "<u>I will</u> help to make our tea," said Ben.

_____

Published by Thomas Nelson and Sons Ltd

unit
6

name _____   date _____

Capital letters

A Draw a circle around all the letters that should be capital letters.

1 "when did david arrive?" asked zoe.

2 "my favourite book is called stig of the dump," said joanne.

3 louise, darren and eva all have birthdays in july.

4 amy and i went to spain on holiday.

5 my best friend lives in south street and i live in western road.

B Copy the book titles below, putting in the missing capital letters for important words.

1 the lion, the witch and the wardrobe

_____

2 the bumper book of puzzles and games

_____

3 recipes for rainy days

_____

4 folk tales of the british isles

_____

5 the cat in the hat

_____

6 a dragon in the ice

_____

unit
6

Published by Thomas Nelson and Sons Ltd

Writing instructions

What are you writing instructions for? _____

What you will need:

_____   _____

_____   _____

_____   _____

What to do:

1 _____

_____

_____

2 _____

_____

_____

3 _____

_____

_____

4 _____

_____

_____

If you have not finished your instructions, turn this sheet over and write on the other side of this sheet.

A card trick

PICK A CARD

What you need:
a pack of playing cards

What to do:

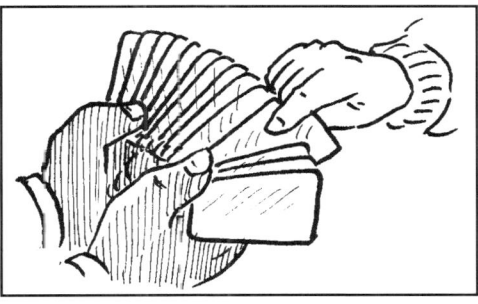

1 Shuffle the pack of cards.

2 Hold out the cards in a fan shape, face downwards.

3 Ask someone to pick out a card without letting you see it.

4 Shuffle the pack again.

5 With your right hand, lift some cards from the top of the pack.

6 Ask the person to put their card face down on top of the cards in your left hand.

7 Quickly glance at the front card in your right hand. Don't let the audience see you do it. Put the pack back together.

8 Turn the cards over one at a time, from the top of the pile.

9 When you come to the card you saw in step 7, you will know the next card is the person's card. You can amaze the audience by correctly picking the card they chose.

unit
6

Pick a card

Take a pack of cards and shuffle them. Ask someone to pick a card and then to put it back in the pack. You need to look at the card their other card has gone next to. Turn the cards over and when you see the card you saw before, you will know what the other card is.

Contractions

A Draw a line to join each pair of words to the correct contraction. The first one has been done to help you.

1	did not		wouldn't
2	would not		I'll
3	I am		mustn't
4	we have		we're
5	you will		here's
6	must not		didn't
7	she will		she'll
8	we are		we've
9	I will		I'm
10	here is		you'll

B Write the contraction for each pair of words.

1 they are _____   2 does not _____

3 it is _____   4 there is _____

5 have not _____   6 it will _____

7 has not _____   8 they will _____

unit 7

Using commas with speech marks

Add the missing speech marks and commas to these sentences. The first one has been done to help you.

1 "I will go myself and meet this Minotaur," said Theseus.

2 I will kill the Minotaur he said.

3 Please be very careful begged his father.

4 I wish you would stay here with me he said.

5 I must kill the monster to stop him killing other people explained Theseus.

6 I have a plan that will help you said Ariadne.

7 You must take this ball of string she explained.

8 Unroll the string as you go through the maze she added.

9 It will help me find my way back said Theseus.

10 What a clever idea he added.

unit 7

Planning the characters in a story

Story title: _____

You are going to make notes about one of the characters in your story.
What is the character's name?

_____

Words to describe what the character looks like:

_____ _____

_____ _____

_____ _____

_____ _____

Words to describe what sort of character he/she is:

_____ _____

_____ _____

_____ _____

_____ _____

You are going to make notes about another character in your story.
What is the character's name?

_____

Words to describe what the character looks like:

_____ _____

_____ _____

_____ _____

_____ _____

Words to describe what sort of character he/she is:

_____ _____

_____ _____

_____ _____

_____ _____

Published by Thomas Nelson and Sons Ltd

Daedalus and Icarus

There is a Greek myth about a man called Daedalus, who was very good at building things. King Minos of Crete had captured Daedalus and his son, Icarus, because he wanted to build a great maze to house the monster known as the Minotaur. King Minos said that Daedalus and Icarus could leave as soon as they had built the maze.

Daedalus was given a workshop in a high tower, and he worked very hard and built an enormous maze. The Minotaur was put in the very middle of the maze. King Minos was very pleased.

Daedalus went to the King and said, "We have finished building the maze. Please keep your promise and let us go free." But King Minos did not keep his promise. He wanted Daedalus to build other things, so he would not let them go.

Daedalus watched the birds from the window in the tower and came up with a plan. He told his son to collect birds' feathers. He stuck together the feathers with hot wax and made two pairs of wings – a pair for Icarus and a pair for himself.

When they were ready to fly out of the high tower, Daedalus said to Icarus, 'You must not fly too low or the spray from the sea will make your wings wet and heavy. You must not fly too high or the sun will melt the wax and your wings will come apart. Stay near me and you will be safe.'

Icarus followed his father out of the window but he did not do as his father had told him. He thought flying was great fun and he went high up into the sky. Soon, the hot sun melted the wax on his wings and the feathers started to fall off. Icarus fell towards the sea and there was nothing Daedalus could do to save the foolish boy.

unit
7

Definitions

Next to each word, write its definition. Use your dictionary to help you. Then, use each word in a sentence of your own.

1 maze

Definition: _____

Sentence: _____

2 amaze

Definition: _____

Sentence: _____

3 confuse

Definition: _____

Sentence: _____

4 deceive

Definition: _____

Sentence: _____

5 dilemma

Definition: _____

Sentence: _____

6 perform

Definition: _____

Sentence: _____

7 destroy

Definition: _____

Sentence: _____

unit
7

Singular and plural sentences

A Copy these sentences, changing them from singular to plural.

1 That boy is good at writing stories.

_____

2 This girl is Peter's sister.

_____

3 She was using the computer.

_____

4 He was moving the ladder when he spilt the paint.

_____

B Copy these sentences, changing them from plural to singular.

1 The girls were careful when they crossed the road.

_____

2 There were some books in those suitcases.

_____

3 The birds are building their nests.

_____

4 Those boys are going to be late.

_____

unit
7

Classroom rules

unit 7

DO

Rule 1

Do _____   Reason _____

_____   _____

_____   _____

Rule 2

Do _____   Reason _____

_____   _____

_____   _____

Rule 3

Do _____   Reason _____

_____   _____

_____   _____

DON'T

Rule 1

Don't _____   Reason _____

_____   _____

_____   _____

Rule 2

Don't _____   Reason _____

_____   _____

_____   _____

Rule 3

Don't _____   Reason _____

_____   _____

_____   _____

A map of Duffington

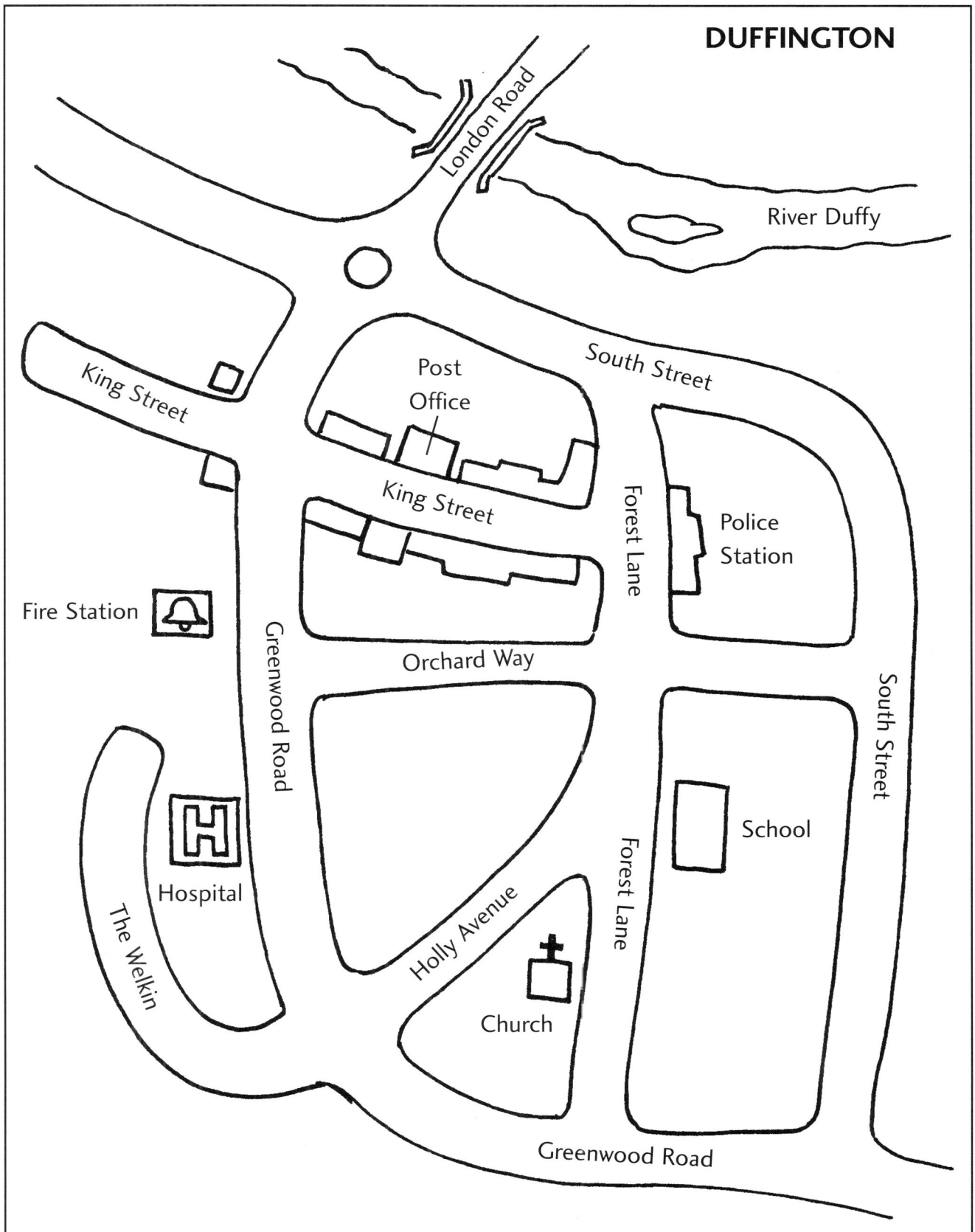

Nelson English © John Jackman and Wendy Wren 2000

Adding 'ing'

A Do these word sums. Remember the rules for adding 'ing'.

1 make + ing = _____

2 bite + ing = _____

3 jump + ing = _____

4 shove + ing = _____

5 drive + ing = _____

6 drop + ing = _____

7 slap + ing = _____

8 smile + ing = _____

9 live + ing = _____

10 grip + ing = _____

11 climb + ing = _____

12 skip + ing = _____

B Write a verb that ends with 'ing' to go with each picture clue.

1 _____ 2 _____ 3 _____

4 _____ 5 _____ 6 _____

unit 8

Collective nouns

A   Write a collective noun to match each picture below.

1 _____

2 _____

3 _____

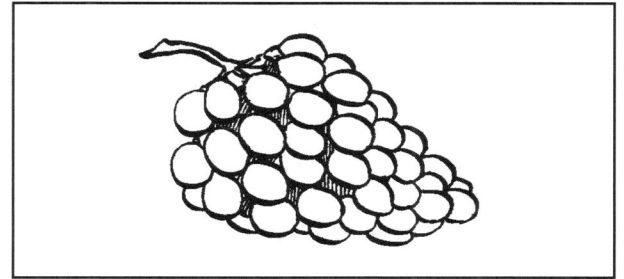

4 _____

5 _____

6 _____

B   Name two things you would find in each of these groups. The first one has been done to help you.

1   pack   _____cards_____   _____wolves_____

2   bunch   _____   _____

3   herd   _____   _____

4   flock   _____   _____

unit
8

Poetry writing

Feet

Feet

Splashing

Stamping in puddles

_____ing and _____ing

_____ing and _____ing

_____ing and _____ing

_____ing and _____ing

_____ing and _____ing

_____ing and _____ing

_____ing and _____ing

_____ing and _____ing

_____ing

_____ing

_____ _____ing

_____

unit **8**

Faces

Faces

Winking

Sleeping in bed

_____ing and _____ing

_____ing and _____ing

_____ing and _____ing

_____ing and _____ing

_____ing and _____ing

_____ing and _____ing

_____ing and _____ing

_____ing and _____ing

_____ing

_____ing

_____ _____ing

_____

King Midas and the Golden Touch

This Roman legend about greedy King Midas shows that you should be very careful what you wish for.

Bacchus was the son of Jupiter, the king of Roman gods. When Bacchus was young, he was looked after by Silenus. Silenus was half man and half goat and, together, he and Bacchus travelled far and wide having fun and adventures.

One day, Silenus got lost. As he was wandering about, he met King Midas, who helped him to find Bacchus. Bacchus was so delighted to see his friend again that he promised King Midas any reward he wanted. Now King Midas was a very greedy man, and immediately he asked that all he touched would be turned into gold. Bacchus granted Midas's wish and he and Silenus went on their way.

King Midas hurried back to his palace to test his new power. He wandered around the palace gardens, touching flowers and statues, all of which turned to gold as soon as his hand touched them. He was so delighted that he told his servants to prepare a great feast and invite everyone to share in his good fortune.

When King Midas sat down at the feast and began to eat, he had a great shock. His plate, his cup, the tablecloth and his food all turned to gold as soon as he touched them! He realised what a foolish thing he had wished for and immediately returned to Bacchus to ask that the young god take back the power he had given him.

Bacchus saw that Midas had learned his lesson and told him to go and bathe in a nearby river if he wished to be rid of the power to turn everything he touched to gold.

Published by Thomas Nelson and Sons Ltd   Nelson English © John Jackman and Wendy Wren 2000

unit 8

Antonyms

A Draw a line to join each underlined word to its antonym. The first one has been done to help you.

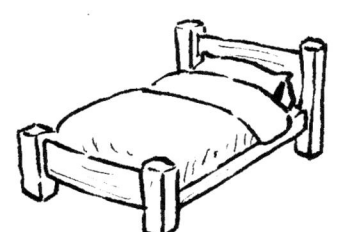

1 a <u>hard</u> bed   on

2 a <u>light</u> colour   soft

3 <u>off</u> the floor   low

4 a <u>sad</u> film   long

5 a <u>high</u> bridge   happy

6 a <u>short</u> story   dark

7 a <u>heavy</u> load   smooth

8 a <u>rough</u> road   light

unit 8

B In each sentence, fill the gap with the antonym of the underlined word.

1 When you are not <u>wet</u>, you are _____.

2 Some of the questions are <u>easy</u>, but others are _____.

3 Summer is <u>hot</u>, but winter is _____.

4 My new coat is <u>clean</u>, but my old one is _____.

5 These sandwiches are <u>stale</u>, but the buns are _____.

6 The answer is either <u>yes</u> or _____.

Published by Thomas Nelson and Sons Ltd

Using 'is', 'was', 'are' and 'were'

A   Complete each sentence by writing 'is' or 'are' in the gap.

1   We _____ visiting Water World.

2   Josh _____ carrying our picnic.

3   Moira and Tara _____ running down to the lake.

4   They _____ going on a speed-boat ride.

5   It _____ fun on the huge water slide.

6   "You _____ soaking!" laughs Dad.

unit
8

B   Write 'was' or 'were' in each gap.

1   It _____ time to go home.

2   They _____ nearly the last to leave.

3   "I _____ the bravest!" said Josh.

4   "You _____ not, I _____ !" said Tara.

5   Moira laughed, "Dad _____ the bravest to bring us!"

6   They all agreed it _____ a fun day out.

Flow diagrams

Complete this flow diagram showing how a tadpole turns into a frog.

What happens on day 1?

_____

_____

_____

What happens on day 3?

_____

_____

_____

What happens at 8–10 weeks?

_____

_____

_____

What happens at 12 weeks?

_____

_____

_____

What happens at 14–16 weeks?

_____

_____

unit 8

Sign language

Sign language is one way that people who cannot hear or who cannot speak use to communicate. They make shapes with their hands, and each shape means something different, like the letters of the alphabet. Lots of hand movements mean whole words or even phrases. Anybody can learn to use sign language.

Here is the sign language alphabet:

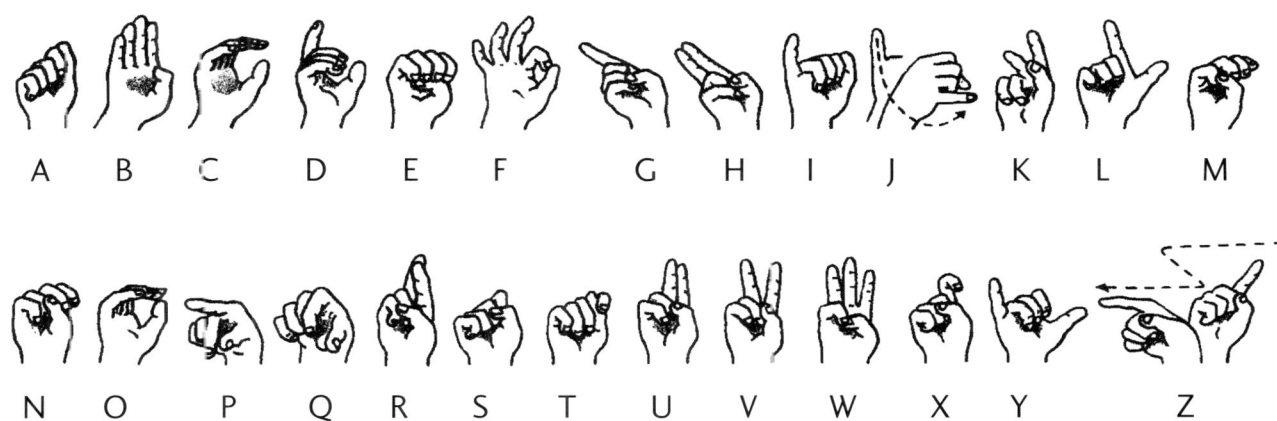

A   B   C   D   E   F   G   H   I   J   K   L   M

N   O   P   Q   R   S   T   U   V   W   X   Y   Z

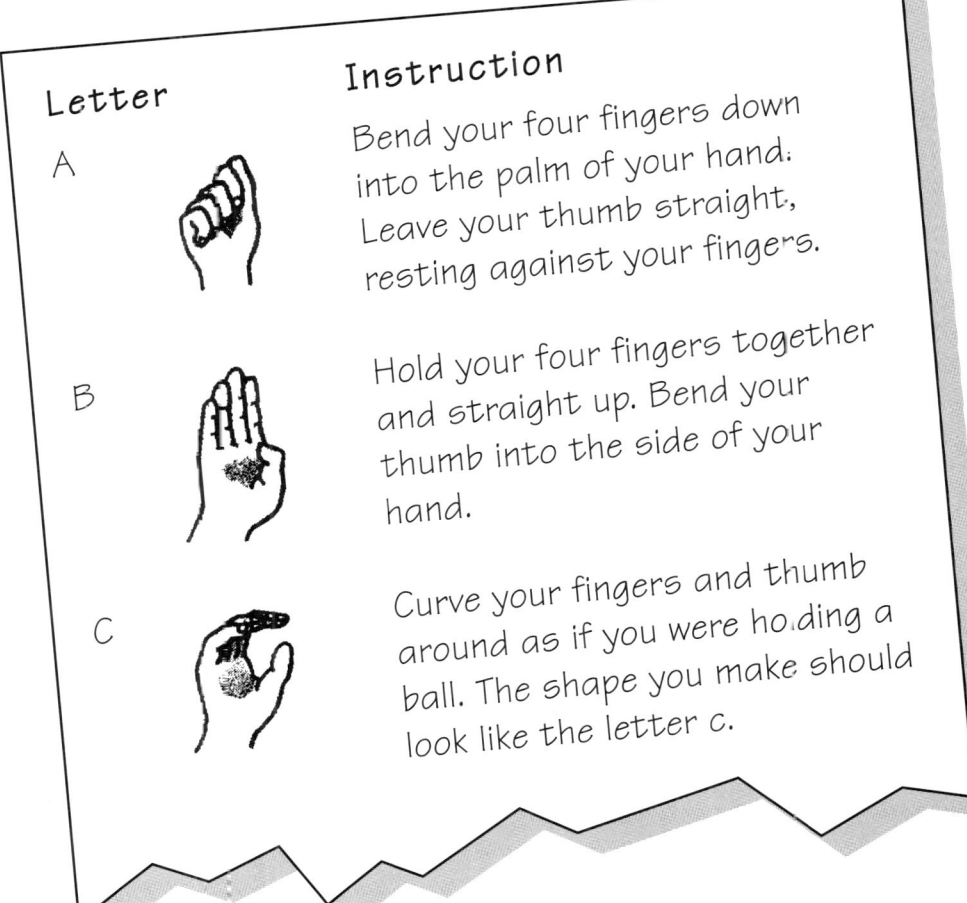

Letter		Instruction
A		Bend your four fingers down into the palm of your hand. Leave your thumb straight, resting against your fingers.
B		Hold your four fingers together and straight up. Bend your thumb into the side of your hand.
C		Curve your fingers and thumb around as if you were holding a ball. The shape you make should look like the letter c.

unit
8

Synonyms – 'said'

The word 'said' has been left out of all the sentences below. Fill each gap with a synonym for 'said'. You could choose words from the box or think of some of your own.

You also need to add the speech marks that have been left out.

laughed	grumbled	warned	promised	cried
shouted	asked	whispered		

1 That's a very funny joke, _____ Gran.

2 Be careful! You'll hurt yourself, _____ Dad.

3 Could you tell me the way to the station? the stranger _____.

4 One more goal and we'll have won! the team captain _____.

5 Don't wake the baby, _____ Mum.

6 That's not fair! I haven't had any cake, _____ Zak.

7 I'll buy you a present in town, _____ Aunty Carol.

8 I've torn my trousers, Billy _____.

Pronouns

A Choose a pronoun from the box to complete each sentence.
The first one has been done to help you.

He	She
They	It

1 __She__ is running.

2 _____ is writing.

3 _____ are cooking.

4 _____ is cutting.

5 _____ is hopping.

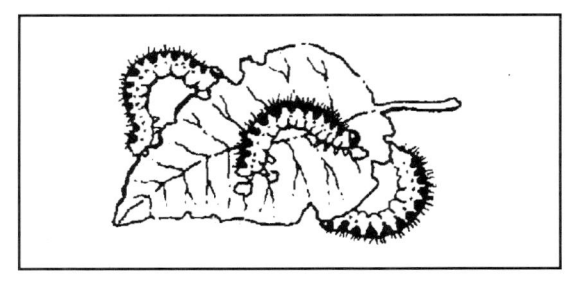

6 _____ are eating.

B Draw a circle around each pronoun in this passage.

Ben and Ella are going on holiday. They are going to visit Billy
in Canada. He is their cousin. Ella has never met him before.
"I am very excited," she said. "I can't wait until we leave."
"It will be lovely to see Billy and Aunty Rita and Uncle Chris
again," said Ben.
"Are they meeting us at the airport?" asked Ella.

unit
9

Writing in the first person

I am the Dormouse. When Alice came to tea …

This is what I saw:

_____   _____
_____   _____
_____   _____

This is what I did:

_____   _____
_____   _____
_____   _____

This is what I said:

_____   _____
_____   _____
_____   _____

unit 9

This is what I thought:

_____
_____
_____
_____
_____

name _____   date _____

My Party

'My Party' by Kit Wright is from *Rabbiting On*, published by HarperCollins, and is reproduced with the permission of Marianne Chipperfield on behalf of the author.

My parents said I could have a party
And that's just what I did.

Dad said, 'Who have you thought of inviting?'
I told him. He said, 'Well, you'd better start
    writing,'
And that's just what I did

To:
Phyllis Willis, Horace Morris,
Nancy, Clancy, Bert and Gert Sturt,
Dick and Mick and Nick Crick,
Ron, Don, John,
Dolly, Molly, Polly –
Neil Peel –
And my dear old friend, Dave Dirt.

I wrote, 'Come along, I'm having a party,'
And that's just what they did.

They all arrived with huge appetites
As Dad and I were fixing the lights.
I said, 'Help yourself to the drinks and bites!'
And that's just what they did,
All of them:
Phyllis Willis, Horace Morris,
Nancy, Clancy, Bert and Gert Sturt,
Dick and Mick and Nick Crick,
Ron, Don, John,
Dolly, Molly, Polly –
Neil Peel –
And my dear old friend, Dave Dirt.

Now, I had a good time and as far as I
    could tell,
The party seemed to go pretty well –
Yes, that's just what it did.

Then Dad said, 'Come on, just for fun,
Let's have a *turn* from everyone!'
And a turn's just what they did,

All of them:

Phyllis Willis, Horace Morris,
Nancy, Clancy, Bert and Gert Sturt,
Dick and Mick and Nick Crick,
Ron, Don, John,
Dolly, Molly, Polly –
Neil Peel –
And my dear old friend, Dave Dirt.

AND THIS IS WHAT THEY DID:

Phyllis and Clancy
And Horace and Nancy
Did a song and dance number
That was really fancy –

Dolly, Molly, Polly,
Ron, Don and John
performed a play
That went on and on and on –

Gert and Bert Sturt,
Sister and brother,
Did an imitation of
Each other.
(Gert Sturt put on Bert Sturt's shirt
And Bert Sturt put on Gert Sturt's skirt.)

Neil Peel
All on his own
Danced an eightsome reel.

Dick and Mick
And Nicholas Crick
Did a most *ingenious*
Conjuring trick

And my dear old friend, Dave Dirt,
Was terribly sick
All over the flowers.
We cleaned it up.
It took *hours*.

But as Dad said, giving a party's not easy.
You really
Have to
Stick at it.
I agree. And if Dave gives a party
I'm certainly
Going to be
Sick at it.

by Kit Wright

unit 9

Words within words

There are lots of words hidden in this word search. The words go from top to bottom and from left to right.

Draw a circle around each word you can find in the word search.
The first one has been done to help you.

b	i	r	t	h	d	a	y	p	w
u	n	o	g	a	m	e	s	r	a
s	v	w	e	p	c	a	k	e	s
s	i	t	t	p	a	r	t	s	m
a	t	e	n	y	o	u	r	e	i
p	a	r	c	e	l	f	u	n	l
b	t	u	b	s	l	o	w	t	e
i	i	b	o	o	t	o	y	s	s
t	o	m	o	r	r	o	w	i	n
e	n	d	k	p	a	r	t	y	o

unit **9**

Pronouns

A Draw a circle round all the personal pronouns and possessive pronouns in this passage.

I told my friend, Megan, that I would miss her while she and her family were away. She said that they were leaving for their holiday on Saturday morning. Her uncle is going to take them to the airport in his new car. My sister and I said we would go round to say goodbye on Friday night if our mum would let us.

B 1 Copy each sentence, replacing the underlined words with pronouns.

   a <u>Megan and her parents</u> were going away for a fortnight.

   _____

   b My sister and I asked <u>Megan</u> to send <u>my sister and me</u> a postcard.

   _____

   c Megan said <u>Megan</u> would miss <u>my sister and me</u>.

   _____

   2 Copy each sentence, replacing the underlined words with possessive pronouns.

   a Megan said that the heaviest suitcase was <u>Megan's</u>.

   _____

   b Her dad said it was twice the size of <u>her dad's</u>.

   _____

   c "Which suitcase is <u>your suitcase</u>?" I asked <u>Megan's</u> mum.

   _____

unit
9

Letters

your address _____

_____

_____

The name of the person you are writing to

today's date _____

Dear _____

Your first paragraph, saying why you are writing the letter.

_____

_____

_____

Your second paragraph, saying what you will do if they come.

_____

_____

_____

unit 9

Your third paragraph, saying you hope they can come.

_____

_____

_____

_____   your friendly ending

_____   your name

A letter of complaint

Seaview Hotel
3 Marine Drive
Farnbury-on-Sea
GH3 27B

14th June

Dear Mr Collins,

As you know, I run a small hotel just across the street from where you live. I have had to write to you before about the noise that comes from your house when you are having a party. You seem to have a lot of parties!

On Saturday, many people arrived at your house and I guessed you were having another party. The noise was not too bad in the early evening but by 11 o'clock, three of the people who were staying at the hotel had complained that there was too much noise coming from across the road. One couple were having trouble getting their child to sleep and another guest, who stays here every summer, could not hear his television.

I am sorry to have to write to you again to complain but, very soon, no one will want to stay at my hotel because of all the noise you make.

I am sure that, when you have read this letter, you will understand the problem and will not have such noisy parties in the future.

Yours sincerely,

Nora Flint

unit
9

Singular and plural nouns

Feed these words through the plural-making machine and write the plurals in the basket underneath.

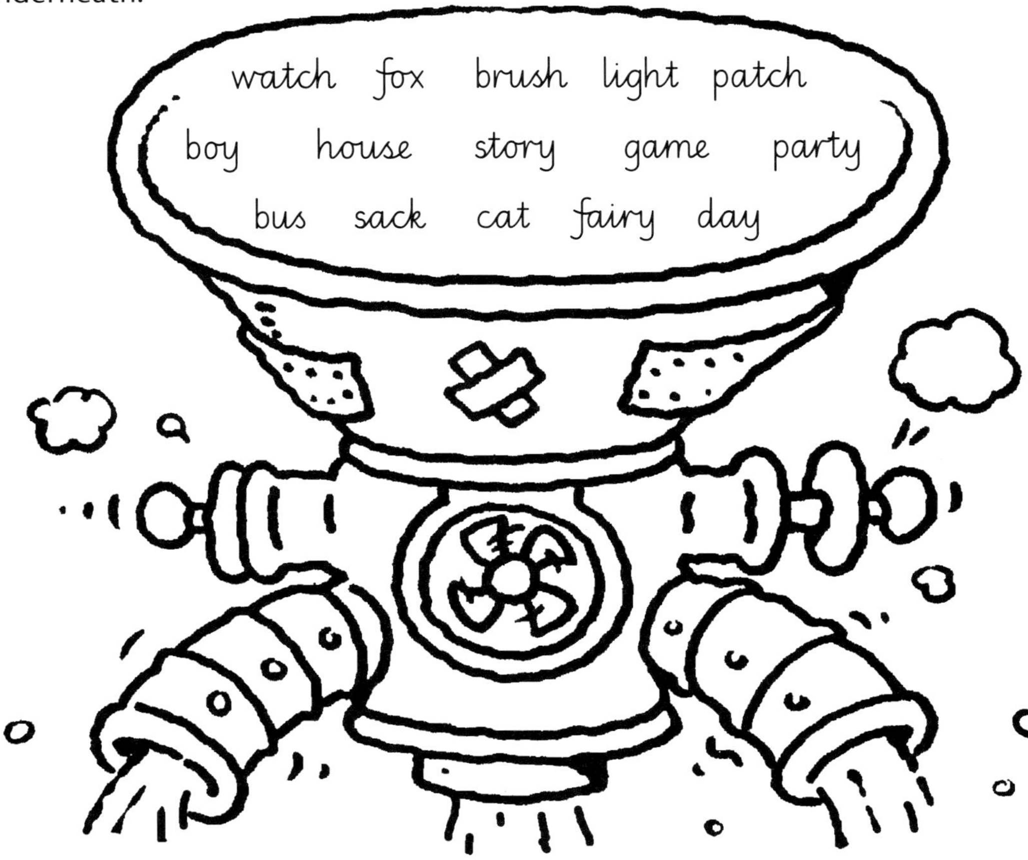

watch   fox   brush   light   patch
boy   house   story   game   party
bus   sack   cat   fairy   day

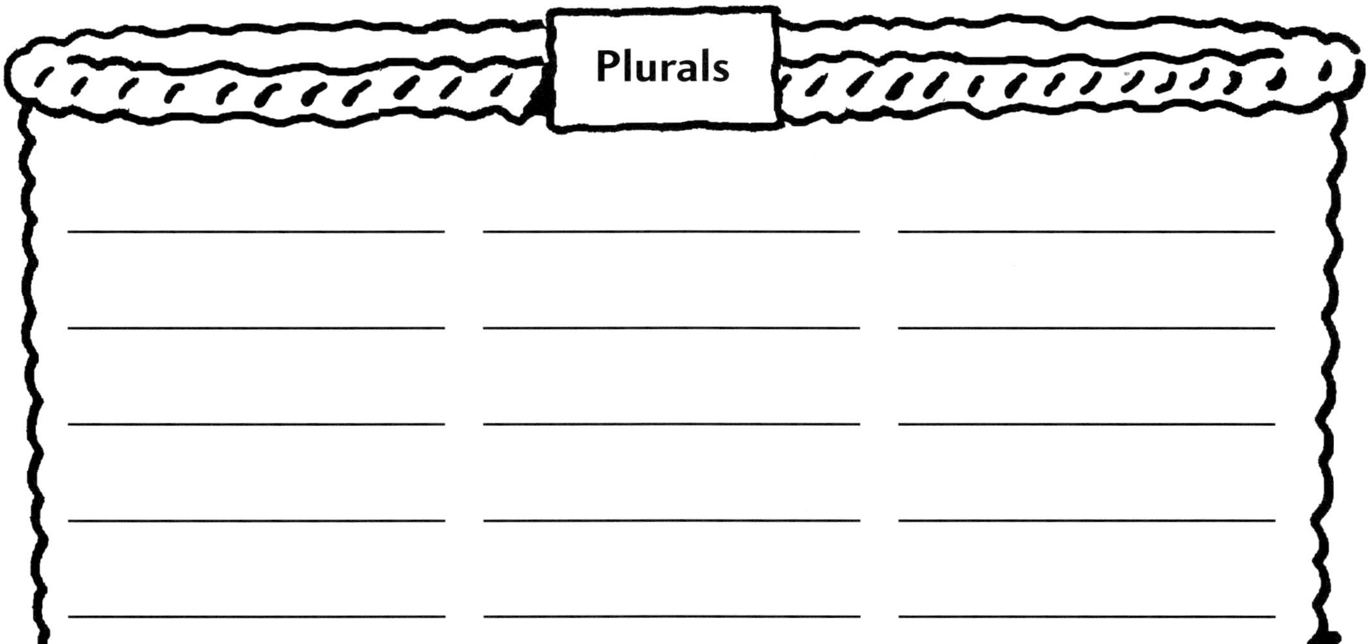

Plurals

_____   _____   _____

_____   _____   _____

_____   _____   _____

_____   _____   _____

Gender words

A   Look at the nouns in the box. They are either male or female.

brother   lord   sister   mare   husband
stallion
lady   boy   boar   Mrs
actress   wife   drake
Mr   actor
nephew   duck   sow   niece   girl

Write each noun in the correct box below. You could use a dictionary to help you.

Male (masculine)	**Female (feminine)**
_____ _____	_____ _____
_____ _____	_____ _____
_____ _____	_____ _____
_____ _____	_____ _____
_____	_____

B   Look at the nouns in the box below. Draw a circle around the nouns that can be both male and female.

father   sister   animal
people
relative   baby
fish
elephant   man   girl
woman
grandfather   headteacher   grandparent
child
doctor   person   headmistress

unit
10

Feelings in stories

What I am writing about: _____

_____

To make the reader feel frightened, I would write it like this:

_____

_____

_____

_____

_____

To make the reader feel sad, I would write it like this:

_____

_____

_____

_____

_____

To make the reader laugh, I would write it like this:

_____

_____

_____

_____

unit
10

Storm

They're at it again
the wind and the rain
It all started
when the wind
took the window
by the collar
and shook it
with all its might
Then the rain
butted in
What a din
they'll be at it all night
Serves them right
if they go home in the morning
and the sky won't let them in

by Roger McGough

'Storm' by Roger McGough is from *After the Merrymaking*, published by Jonathan Cape Ltd. Reprinted by permission of The Peters Fraser and Dunlop Group Limited on behalf of Roger McGough. © Roger McGough.

unit
10

Adjectives

A Draw a circle around the word that you would use to describe the person or animal that is wearing a hat in each picture.

1 dirty   dirtier   dirtiest

2 successful   more successful

3 heavy   heavier

4 happy   happier   happiest

B Complete this table of comparative and superlative adjectives.

adjective	comparative	superlative
cold	colder	coldest
large		
funny		
pretty		
wet		
sunny		
late		
wonderful		
important		

unit **10**

First, second and third person

A   Write whether each sentence is in the first person, second person or third person.

1   I went to bed very early last night.   _____

2   The natural history club will meet on Monday.   _____

3   None of the pupils knew whether they had passed the test. _____

4   You must remember to take the dog to the vet tomorrow.   _____

5   When I got to the shop, it was closed.   _____

6   When you arrive, please come to my office.   _____

B   1   Copy each sentence, changing it to be in the first person. You need to change the underlined words.

a   <u>The girl</u> fell down the steps.

_____

b   <u>The boy</u> had not finished <u>his</u> homework.

_____

2   Copy each sentence, changing it to be in the second person. You need to change the underlined words.

a   <u>She</u> has forgotten <u>her</u> coat.

_____

b   <u>I</u> missed <u>my</u> train.

_____

3   Copy each sentence, changing it to be in the third person. You need to change the underlined words.

a   <u>Your</u> family only just reached the airport in time.

_____

b   <u>Our</u> teacher asked <u>us</u> to tidy the classroom.

_____

unit 10

Making notes for a report

What is your report about? _____

Write a list of the things that happened, in the correct order.

_____

_____

_____

_____

Write some words and phrases you could use to describe what happened.

_____

_____

_____

_____

Write some words and phrases you could use to describe the people.

_____

_____

_____

_____

Now write your report. Use the back of this sheet if you need more space.

_____

_____

_____

_____

_____

_____

_____

_____

_____

unit
10

name _____   date _____

Cyclones

Cyclones are great winds, sometimes called hurricanes, They are far more powerful than any strong wind that we have in Britain. They can cause terrible damage and sometimes injure and kill thousands of people. They often occur in the Caribbean and in the Indian Ocean.

The very powerful winds of a cyclone can last several days, and usually bring torrential rain, which often causes flooding or mudslides, which can do further damage. Weather forecasters find it difficult to know where cyclones will move to next. People living in areas that might be in the path of a cyclone are usually warned that they may be in danger. They may leave the area and stay somewhere safer until the cyclone has passed, or they may stay in their homes, boarding up the windows and trying to protect their possessions from the wind.

Cyclones or hurricanes are usually first spotted from satellite photographs (photographs taken from space). They can be seen because they make huge spiral-shaped cloud patterns as the winds spin faster and faster.

There are many different types of strong wind. Here are some of the commonest:

hurricane:	a storm with a violent wind, especially a tropical cyclone in the Caribbean
monsoon:	a strong wind in South Asia
tempest:	a violent windy storm
tornado:	a small, violent cyclone in which the air spirals inwards and upwards at high speed
typhoon:	a tropical storm in the western Pacific
willy-willy:	a cyclone or dust storm in Australia

unit
10

name _____ date _____

Root words

A 1 Make new words by adding the suffix 'ful' or 'ly' to the end of each root word.

a pain_____

b sad_____

c hope_____

d quick_____

e care_____

f love_____

2 Make new words by adding the prefix 'un' or 'dis' to the beginning of each root word.

a _____load

b _____safe

c _____honest

d _____usual

e _____wise

f _____trust

B Choose four root words from part A. For each word, write down four other words from the same word family. For example:

sad_____ : saddest_____ sadden_____ sadder_____ sadness_____

1 _____ : _____ _____ _____ _____

2 _____ : _____ _____ _____ _____

3 _____ : _____ _____ _____ _____

4 _____ : _____ _____ _____ _____

unit
11

Conjunctions

A Draw a line under each of the two short sentences that were put together to make each of the sentences below. Draw a circle around the conjunction that was used to join them.

1 The sand is warm but the water is cold.

2 The wind blew strongly and the sand went into my eyes.

3 Mum carried our lunch and we carried the chairs.

4 I made a sandcastle, but the waves washed it away.

B Use 'and' or 'but' to join each pair of sentences.

1 Take your bucket. Get some water from the sea.

_____

2 They must not swim near the rocks. They can swim near the beach.

_____

_____

3 Everyone had great fun at the beach. We are all very tired now.

_____

_____

unit
11

name _____   date _____

Book reviews

| Title _____ |
| Author _____ |

The story is about _____

_____

_____

_____

_____

It is set in _____

_____

_____

_____

_____

One of the characters is _____

_____

_____

_____

_____

My opinion of the story is _____

_____

_____

_____

_____

unit 11

Book blurbs

The owl-tree is not like any tree Joe has ever seen. It's huge and leafy and shivers at times like a person; it even seems to speak. Granny Diamond once saw an owl perched among its branches and she has loved the tree ever since. It means the world to her. But her neighbour, Mr Rock, wants to cut it down. Why does he dislike the owl-tree so much? Does the tree have a secret to tell Joe? And how can he, a boy too scared even to *climb* the tree, be the one to save it?

The Owl-Tree

by Jenny Nimmo

How wonderful to find a magic carpet in your house. Even more mysterious is the two-thousand-year-old bird, the Phoenix, who accompanies it. This beautiful yet peculiar bird teaches the four adventurous children how to travel to exotic places on the magic carpet. They only have to wish and they are whisked to the South Sea Islands or to Indian bazaars, whilst always keeping one wish for emergencies!

The Phoenix and the Carpet

by E Nesbit

The sun rose higher. On they walked. The heat sank into them and they felt the sweat on their bodies. On they walked. Alone again …

Naledi had made up her mind. Dineo was ill and needed her mother, but she worked and lived 300 miles away in Johannesburg. The only way to let her know was to get to the big road and walk. So Naledi and her brother Tiro did just that …

Journey to Jo'burg

by Beverley Naidoo

unit
11

    Nelson English © John Jackman and Wendy Wren 2000

Using a dictionary

Each page of a dictionary has **guide words** to show you the first word and the last word that appear on that page.

A Here are the guide words for three pages in a dictionary.
Write on the correct page below each word from the box.

marsh – muddle	**break – catch**
_____	_____
_____	_____
_____	_____
_____	_____
_____	_____
_____	_____

poison – quest	
_____	mast puddle
_____	brother brush
_____	practise mud
_____	Moon candle
_____	quality mile
_____	build purchase
_____	porridge meal
	carriage

B Add two more words to each page above.

Conjunctions

A Use a conjunction to join each pair of sentences.

1 We have to write a report about the Romans. I am going to the library to find some books.

_____

_____

2 We must use an encyclopedia for research. We must also use other information books.

_____

_____

B 1 Write three short sentences about this picture.

_____

_____

_____

2 Now join the three short sentences to make one longer sentence, using conjunctions.

_____

_____

_____

unit
11

Using a library

What would a non-fiction book with the number 53 be about?

_____

Write the book title here

Write the author's name here

What would a non-fiction book with the number 56 be about?

_____

Write the book title here

Write the author's name here

What would a non-fiction book with the number 59 be about?

_____

Write the book title here

Write the author's name here

unit 11

Writing and printing

Long ago, not everybody could read and write. When people wanted something written down, they had to get somebody else to do it for them. Books were valuable because it took a very long time to write out a book. When printing methods were invented, lots of copies could be made of a piece of text, so more people could see it.

When we write, we use a pen or a pencil to make marks on a piece of paper. Other people recognise and understand these marks. Printing means that pictures and words can be repeated over and over again without having to be copied out by hand many times.

Words are printed in the same way as fingerprints or footprints. Ink is pressed onto a piece of paper, making a mark.

When printing began, wooden blocks were used. Part of each block was cut away, leaving the words or pictures sticking up. The blocks were then covered in ink and pressed down on to the paper. This is how potato printing works.

Cutting the blocks of wood for printing took a long time. In the middle of the fifteenth century, metal letters were made. These letters could be arranged to make words. Once the words had been printed, the letters could be moved around to make other words. This made printing much quicker.

unit
11

Synonyms

A Write each word from the box in the correct word web.

stroll	beat	chat	snivel	punch	sob	amble
	strike	gossip	weep	stride	speak	

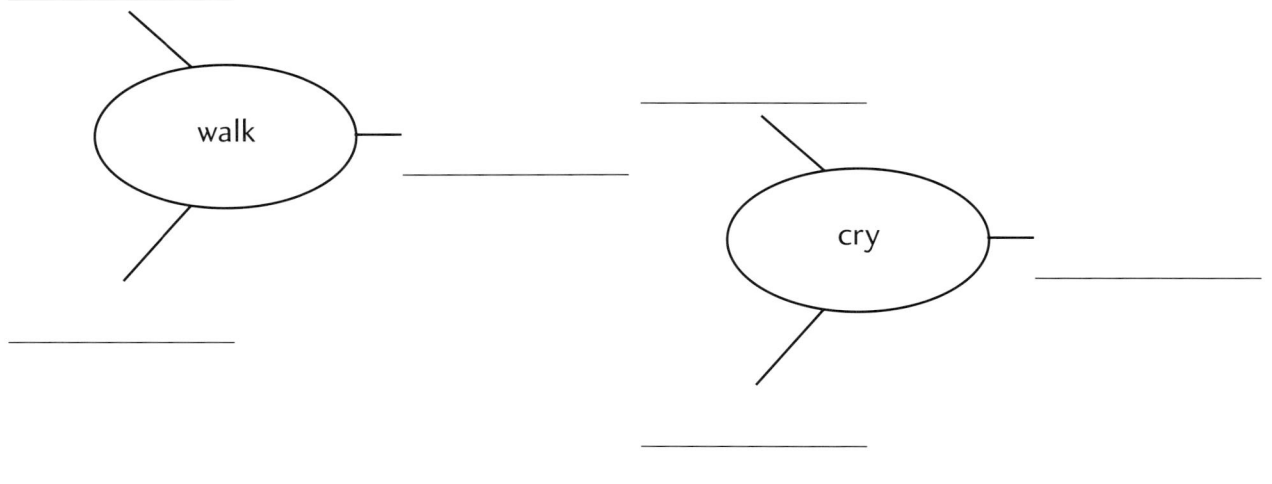

_____

(walk)

_____

_____

(cry)

_____

_____

(talk)

_____

_____

(hit)

_____

B Write two synonyms for each word below.

1 run _____ _____

2 happy _____ _____

3 think _____ _____

4 throw _____ _____

Sentence Level Copymaster 12   Book 1: Fiction

name _____ date _____

Order and time words

A Complete each sentence about the race.

Wesley came _____.

_____ came second.

Peter came _____.

Anna came _____.

_____ came fifth.

Jamie came _____.

_____ came seventh.

Vicky came _____.

Sarah came_____.

_____ came tenth.

B Use words from the box to complete these instructions for cleaning a car.

1 _____, fill a bucket with hot, soapy water.

2 _____ fetch a sponge.

3 _____, wash the car with the soapy water.

4 _____ you have removed all the dirt, fetch a bucket of clean water.

5 Rinse the car _____ all the soap has gone.

6 _____, dry the car with a clean cloth.

| Then |
| until |
| First   Next |
| Finally |
| When |

unit
12

Writing poetry

Complete the first three verses below, then write a fourth verse of your own. Draw some pictures in the gaps, to go with your poem.

I'd like to be a _____

And stay at home all day,

And talk to other _____

In a _____ sort of way.

I'd love to be a _____

And _____

And never _____

Or _____

I wouldn't have to _____

No _____, _____ or _____

I'd just stay _____

And _____

_____

_____

_____

_____

Published by Thomas Nelson and Sons Ltd

The Sound Collector

A stranger called this morning
Dressed all in black and grey
Put every sound into a bag
And carried them away

The whistling of the kettle
The turning of the lock
The purring of the kitten
The ticking of the clock

The popping of the toaster
The crunching of the flakes
When you spread the marmalade
The scraping noise it makes

The hissing of the frying-pan
The ticking of the grill
The bubbling of the bathtub
As it starts to fill

The drumming of the raindrops
On the window-pane
When you do the washing-up
The gurgle of the drain

The crying of the baby
The squeaking of the chair
The swishing of the curtain
The creaking of the stair

A stranger called this morning
He didn't leave his name
Left us only silence
Life will never be the same.

by Roger McGough

'The Sound Collector' by Roger McGough, from *Pillowtalk*, (Penguin 1990) is reprinted by permission of The Peters Fraser and Dunlop Group Limited on behalf of Roger McGough. Copyright © Roger McGough, 1990.

unit
12

Letter blends

A Join each letter blend to the five word endings to make five words.

1

st

- all _____
- art _____
- ay _____
- eam _____
- ill _____

2

str

- ing _____
- eam _____
- ain _____
- aw _____
- ike _____

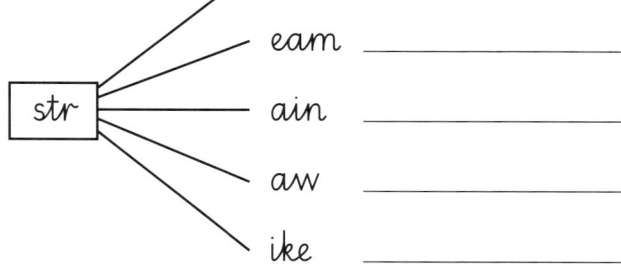

3

sp

- ace _____
- oon _____
- eak _____
- ark _____
- eech _____

4

spr

- ain _____
- ing _____
- ay _____
- ead _____
- out _____

B Add two more words of your own that begin with each letter blend.

1 st _____ _____

2 str _____ _____

3 sp _____ _____

4 spr _____ _____

Published by Thomas Nelson and Sons Ltd

Nouns, adjectives and verbs

Complete the labels for these sentences, saying whether each word is a noun, a verb or an adjective.

1   Granny drank strong tea.

2   Ben ate sticky buns.

3   Dad washed the dirty mugs in some hot water.

4   The naughty baby threw yellow custard all around the room.

5   Sally made a huge sandwich.

Writing an index

Here are the names of the planets around the Sun.

Earth	Mars	Jupiter
Saturn	Uranus	Venus
Mercury	Pluto	Neptune

In a book called *The Planets* you can read about the planets on the following pages.

page 5: Earth, Mars	page 7: Saturn	page 8: Uranus
page 10: Mercury, Venus	page 15: Earth	page 17: Jupiter, Venus
page 18: Neptune	page 19: Mars	page 21: Pluto
page 22: Saturn, Jupiter	page 23: Neptune, Pluto	

Below, make an index for the book. The first entry has been done to help you.

	Page number:
Earth	_5, 15_

Published by Thomas Nelson and Sons Ltd

Glossary

tea	The name given to: 1 an evergreen plant, the leaves of which can be used to make a drink; 2 a drink made from the leaves of the tea plant; 3 an afternoon snack or meal, often served with a cup of tea.
tea bag	A small bag of tea leaves that has many tiny holes. Boiling water is poured over a tea bag to make a cup of tea.
tea break	A short break from work, when you might have a drink, such as a cup of tea.
tea caddy	A container for storing tea.
tea cosy	A cover that is put over a teapot to keep the tea warm.
teapot	A pot in which tea is made. A teapot has a handle, a lid and a spout, and tea can be poured from it into cups or mugs.
tea rose	A flower belonging to the rose family, which smells a bit like tea.
teaspoon	A small spoon, often used for stirring tea.
tea trolley	A trolley with wheels, on which cups, saucers, a teapot and other things needed for serving tea can be moved around.

unit
12

Nelson English

PAGE	MARK
Total:	

BOOK 1
ASSESSMENT PAPER

Reading Comprehension
Homes

INSTRUCTIONS

Questions and Answers

On these sheets, there are different types of questions for you to answer in different ways. The space for your answer shows you what type of writing is needed.

- **one-line answers**
  Some questions are followed by one line.
  This shows that you need only write a word or phrase in your answer.

- **several-line answers**
  Some questions are followed by a few lines.
  This gives you space to write a sentence or two.

- **multiple-choice answers**
  There are some questions where you need to do no writing at all. You need to choose the word or group of words that you think answers the question, and put a ring around your choice.

Please wait until you are told to start work. You should work through the sheets until you are asked to stop.

First Name _____

Last Name _____

Date _____

Published by Thomas Nelson and Sons Ltd

Fiction

Carefully read the passage on each sheet, and then answer the
questions below before moving on to the next sheet.

A Special Place for Edward James

Edward James wanted a special place of his own. First, he tried to make a
special place for himself in the attic. But the attic was full of dusty boxes
and parcels. The sun only shone in for a little time each day. It was a
gloomy place, and no one wants a special place that is gloomy.

Next, he tried to make a
special place in the shed. But
a big spider lived in the shed.
It had woven a beautiful web
for its own special place; and
no matter how hard he tried
not to be, Edward James was
a little afraid of spiders.

1. At first, Edward James tried to make his special place in:

    (a box)   (the attic)   (the shed)

2. What was wrong with the attic?

    _____

    _____

    _____

3. What was wrong with the shed?

    _____

    _____

Total

2

Published by Thomas Nelson and Sons Ltd   Nelson Engl sh © John Jackman and Wendy Wren 2000
The extract from A Special Place for Edward James, by Shirley Isherwood, is reproduced by permission of Andrew Mann Ltd.

Florence tried to make him a special place; a tent made from old curtains. But the tent always fell down, and always when Edward James was inside it.

Mr Manders saw all this, and felt a little sad. He remembered when he was a small bear, and had a special place of his own; a little wooden house, built in a tree. When he sat in it, he could see the sun shining through the gaps in the roof, and he could hear the sound of singing birds, as they flew to and fro among the branches. When the wind blew it made a sound in the tree like the sound of the sea.

4. Why did Mr Manders feel sad?

_____

_____

5. What had been Mr Manders's special place?

_____

_____

6. What did the wind sound like as it blew through the tree?

_____

Total

Published by Thomas Nelson and Sons Ltd   Nelson English © John Jackman and Wendy Wren 2000
The extract from *A Special Place for Edward James*, by Shirley Isherwood, is reproduced by permission of Andrew Mann Ltd.

Every small bear should have a tree house, thought Mr Manders, and he decided that he would make one for Edward James. He would make it that night, so that when Edward James got up the next morning there it would be, with its shining window and its door with a round brass knob. 'And I'll make a sign for the door,' said Mr Manders to himself. 'A sign with his full name: Edward James Fortesque.'

That night, as soon as Edward James was asleep, Mr Manders brought the wood from the shed and began to saw up the planks to make the tree house. The noise of the saw sounded very loud in the still night air – *zit-zat zit-zat*. Mr Manders felt sure that it would wake Edward James, and he crept back into the house to see if he was still asleep.

7. What did Mr Manders decide to do?

   _____

8. Why do you think Mr Manders did not tell Edward James what he planned to do?

   _____

   _____

Total

4

Published by Thomas Nelson and Sons Ltd   Nelson English © John Jackman and Wendy Wren 2000

The extract from *A Special Place for Edward James*, by Shirley Isherwood, is reproduced by permission of Andrew Mann Ltd.

Edward James hardly stirred beneath his patchwork quilt. He was lying flat on his back, and he was fast asleep. Mr Manders went back to the garden, and began to saw his wood again. The noise woke Florence, and she came hurrying down the path in her dressing gown. 'What on earth are you doing, Mr Manders?' she asked.

'I'm making a tree house for Edward James,' said Mr Manders. 'It's going to be very special, with a window and a door with a brass door knob, and his full name on the sign: Edward James Fortesque.'

9. What does the writer mean when she says that Edward James had 'hardly stirred'?

_____

_____

10. Who was woken by the sound of the sawing?

(Edward James)   (Mr Manders)   (Florence)

11. Make a list of the things Mr Manders was planning to include in the tree house.

_____

_____

_____

_____

Total

5

Published by Thomas Nelson and Sons Ltd   Nelson English © John Jackman and Wendy Wren 2000

The extract from *A Special Place for Edward James*, by Shirley Isherwood, is reproduced by permission of Andrew Mann Ltd.

To Mr Manders's surprise, Florence thought that this was a good idea. 'All small bears should have a tree house,' she said firmly. 'I shall make him some cushions and some curtains.' She trotted back down the path, and soon all the lights in the summer house came on. Mr Manders heard the sound of the sewing machine, whirring away.

Mr Manders climbed the tree, and began to haul up the planks of wood on a piece of rope. The branches of the tree creaked loudly. I'm sure that Edward James has woken up, thought Mr Manders. He climbed down from the tree, ran into the house, and peeped into Edward James's bedroom. Edward James had turned on his side, but he was still fast asleep.

---

12. How do you know that Mr Manders thought Florence would not like the tree house?

_____

_____

13. What was Florence going to make for the tree house?

_____

14. Why did the branches of the tree creak loudly?

_____

_____

Total

6

Published by Thomas Nelson and Sons Ltd   Nelson English © John Jackman and Wendy Wren 2000
The extract from *A Special Place for Edward James*, by Shirley Isherwood, is reproduced by permission of Andrew Mann Ltd.

Mr Manders went back into the garden. He was beginning to feel rather tired, and he sat for a moment on a branch. As he sat he watched the long grass of the field stir, as the night animals ran to and from. He felt it would be very pleasant to sit there until the sun came up; but he thought how pleased Edward James would be when he saw his tree house, with its shining window and its door with the brass door knob, and the sign which said, 'Edward James Fortesque'.

He began to nail the walls and the floor of the tree house together. Bang! Bang! Bang! went the hammer. From the summer house there still came the loud whirr of the sewing machine.

15. Why do you think Mr Manders was beginning to feel tired?

_____

_____

_____

16. Why didn't he just sit on the branch until the sun came up?

_____

_____

_____

Total

7

Published by Thomas Nelson and Sons Ltd   Nelson English © John Jackman and Wendy Wren 2000

The extract from *A Special Place for Edward James*, by Shirley Isherwood, is reproduced by permission of Andrew Mann Ltd.

All these noises must have woken Edward James, thought Mr Manders, and he climbed down from the tree and hurried to Edward James's bedroom. Edward James was lying on his tummy with his bottom in the air, and he was still fast asleep.

Mr Manders went back to the garden, and began to climb the tree again. When he reached the first branch he sat down, and he thought about how beautiful the house would be, with its shining window and its door with the brass door knob, and the sign that said, 'Edward James Fortesque'. Thinking of this, he fell asleep, and dreamt that the house was finished, and that they were all having a party inside; himself, and Florence, and Edward James, and three pink pigs …

17. What did Mr Manders dream about?

_____

_____

_____

18. Make a list of all the noises in the story that Mr Manders thought would wake Edward James.

_____

_____

_____

Total

8

Published by Thomas Nelson and Sons Ltd   Nelson English © John Jackman and Wendy Wren 2000

The extract from *A Special Place for Edward James*, by Shirley Isherwood, is reproduced by permission of Andrew Mann Ltd.

Non-fiction

Carefully read the passage on each sheet, and then answer the questions below before moving on to the next sheet.

Building a house

Before a new house can be built, an architect has to draw up some plans. The plans show the builders exactly what the house should look like, and the size, shape and position of the windows, doors and all the rooms.

Next, the site has to be cleared and levelled by bulldozers. Trenches for the foundations are dug by a mechanical digger. The main pipes that will be used for drainage are put in at the same time.

The trenches for the foundations are filled with concrete. Concrete is made by mixing together sand, cement, chippings and water. Sometimes the concrete is brought to the site already mixed in a special lorry. When it is dry, the cement is hard and strong.

---

1. The plans for a house are drawn by:

    (a builder)   (an architect)   (a decorator)

2. What happens once the bulldozers have levelled the site?

    _____

3. What is concrete made from?

    _____

    _____

Total

2

The walls of the house are built on the hard concrete foundations, so that they do not sink into the soft earth. Bricklayers lay rows of bricks, or concrete blocks, on top of each other to make the walls. The bricks or blocks are held together by mortar, which is made by mixing together sand, cement and water.

As the walls are built, holes are left for the windows and doors, and the frames for these are put into position. As the walls get higher, platforms made from scaffolding are put up beside the walls, for the builders to stand on.

___

4. What would happen if the walls were not built on concrete foundations?

_____

_____

5. What is mortar, and what is it used for?

_____

_____

6. Why do builders need scaffolding when they are building a house?

_____

Total

Published by Thomas Nelson and Sons Ltd   Nelson English © John Jackman and Wendy Wren 2000

Once the walls are nearly finished, the roof is made. A framework of wooden roof trusses is covered with slates or tiles, to make the roof waterproof.

When the roof is on and the doors and windows have been fitted, the building is protected from rain. At this stage, electricians can fix the cables that will carry electricity to the house, and plumbers can put in the pipes that will carry clean water into the house and dirty water away.

7. What do you think roof trusses are?

_____

_____

8. Why do you think electricians wait until the roof is tiled before putting in the electricity cables?

_____

_____

Total

4

Next, the ceilings are put up and the walls are plastered, and allowed to dry.

Before the house is finished, plumbers have to put in baths, sinks and lavatories, and a central heating system, carpets and kitchen units may be fitted. Many new homes will also need gas pipes for cookers or central heating systems.

Finally, the electricians come back to fix all the lights, switches and power points and decorators paint the walls, doors and windows, while all the mess and rubbish are cleared away outside.

9. Why do you think the electricity cables are put in before the walls are plastered?

_____

_____

10. Write 1, 2, 3, 4 or 5 in each box to show the order in which the following stages happen:

☐ the roof is tiled

☐ the foundations are dug

☐ the walls are built

☐ decorators paint the windows and doors

☐ the walls are plastered

Total

5

Nelson English © John Jackman and Wendy Wren 2000

Nelson English

WRITING TEST

Fiction – Story writing

Homes

> Choose one of the following story starting points.

1. **The Strange House**
   Write a story called *The Strange House*.

   You should think about:
   - why the house is strange
   - who lives there, or whether it is empty

2. **Moving Day**
   Write a story about a family moving to a new home and lots of things going wrong.

   You should think about:
   - who is in the story
   - what sort of house or flat the family are moving into
   - what sort of things might go wrong

3. **The Crooked House**
   Write a story about this house.

   You should think about:
   - why the house is crooked
   - who lives there

1

Published by Thomas Nelson and Sons Ltd

Story Planning Sheet

Have you chosen **one** of the starting points? Tick the one you have chosen.

☐ The Strange House

☐ Moving Day

☐ The Crooked House

This space is for planning your short story. Look again at the ideas to think about on page 1. Write **very brief notes** about your story. Think about:

- the plot – what is going to happen in your story?
- the characters – who is in your story?
- the setting – where and when does your story take place?
- an opening – how will your story begin?
- an ending – how will your story end?

Your notes will not be marked.

2

Published by Thomas Nelson and Sons Ltd   Nelson English © John Jackman and Wendy Wren 2000

Nelson English

WRITING TEST

Non-fiction – Information writing

Homes

Imagine that somebody who lives in another part of the world wants to know what homes are like in Britain. You are going to write a description of a house or a flat. It could be the home of a friend or relative, or it could be where you live yourself. You need to know quite a lot about the house or flat, because you are going to write down as much information as possible about it.

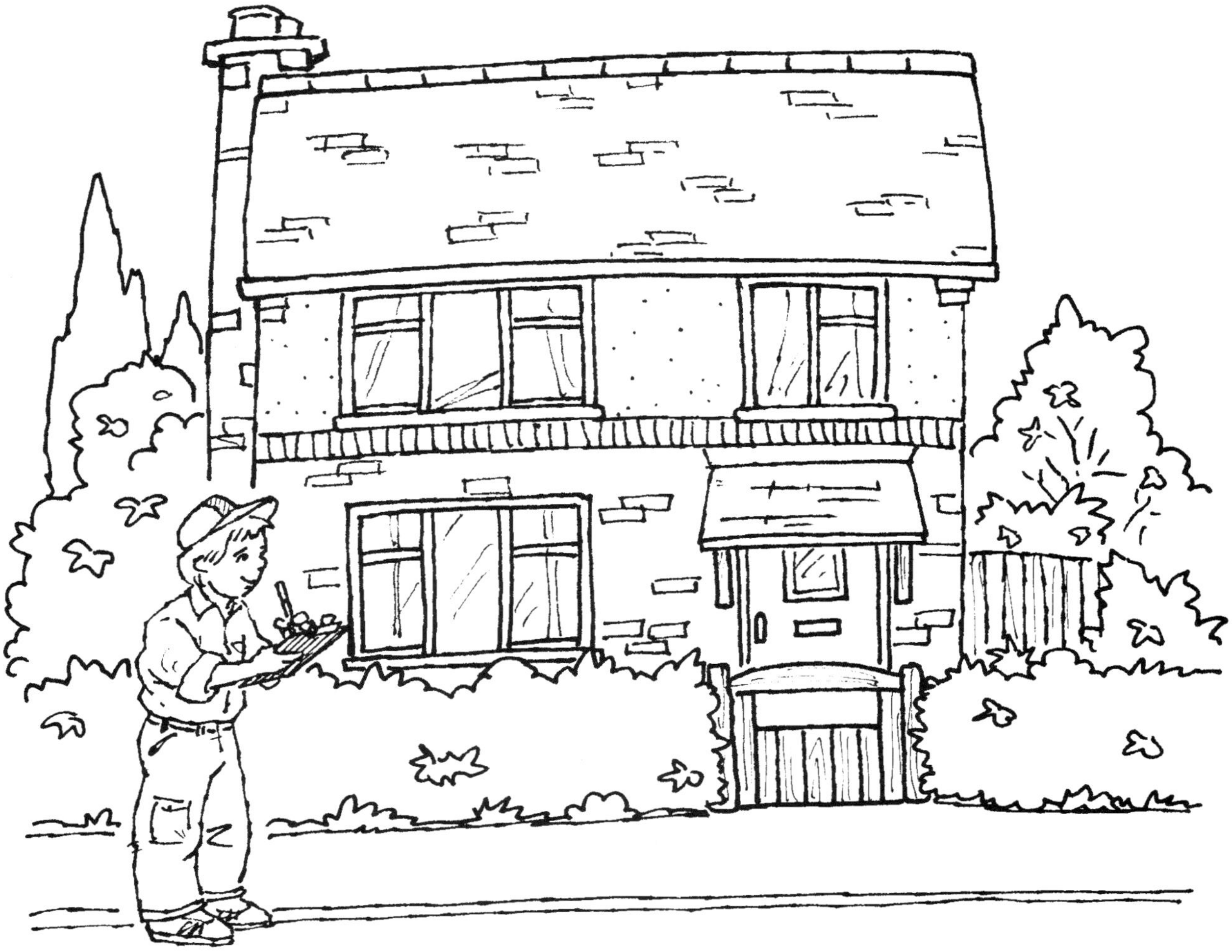

1

Information Planning Sheet

This is for **very brief notes** to help you plan your report.

Your report should state:
- where the house or flat is
- who lives there
- how big/small the house or flat is
- how many rooms there are and how they are arranged
- how the house or flat is heated
- what sort of furniture there is
- how the kitchen is set out
- what sort of equipment the house or flat contains
- any other information you think would be interesting.

Your notes will not be marked.

2

Published by Thomas Nelson and Sons Ltd

Nelson English © John Jackman and Wendy Wren 2000

Nelson English

SPELLING
Teacher's Sheet

First, ask the children to listen as you read through the passage below. Then, read the passage again, much more slowly, stopping at each word the children are to fill in on their copymaster and allowing a pause for them to write. Repeat the word as many times as is necessary. Check that all the children have written the word before continuing.

When the Romans **came** to Britain **just** over 2,000 years ago, they found the Britons **living** in **small** huts. Instead of using **stone** walls, these Britons first set up a **ring** of posts. To make the **roof**, poles were tied from the tops of the posts to a tall, upright post in the centre. The roofs **were** often thatched with reeds.

The **walls** were made of interwoven sticks, called wattle. This was then covered with **clay**. Each group of huts was surrounded by a **fence** and a **ditch**.

The Romans **knew** how to build **bigger** houses, using stone or brick. **Their** country homes were called *villas* and the roofs were usually tiled. Each villa had **several** rooms and was built around an **open** courtyard.

The insides of the walls were **usually** covered with plaster. They often had pictures **painted** on them. The floors of the villa were **often** covered with patterns made from pieces of coloured tile set in cement. These were **called** mosaics.

Nelson English

Spelling Test

First Name _____

Last Name _____

Date _____

When the Romans _____ to Britain _____ over
2,000 years ago, they found the Britons _____ in
huts. Instead of using _____ walls, these Britons first set
up a _____ of posts. To make the _____ , poles
were tied from the tops of the posts to a tall, upright post in
the centre. The roofs _____ often thatched with reeds.

The _____ were made of interwoven sticks, called wattle.
This was then covered with _____. Each group of huts
was surrounded by a _____ and a _____.

The Romans _____ how to build _____ houses,
using stone or brick. _____ country homes were called
villas and the roofs were usually tiled. Each villa had _____
rooms and was built around an _____ courtyard.

The insides of the walls were _____ covered with plaster.
They often had pictures _____ on them. The floors of the
villa were _____ covered with patterns made from pieces
of coloured tile set in cement. These were _____ mosaics.

Total

Published by Thomas Nelson and Sons Ltd

Nelson English
Pupil Record Sheet
Book 1 Year 3

Last name _____

First name _____

Key

⊠ (crossed box, outlined)	Activity undertaken
⊠ (crossed box)	Activity undertaken and understood
⊠ (filled box)	Activity revisited and understood

Title	F/NF	Unit	COMPREHENSION A	COMPREHENSION B	COMPREHENSION C	VOCABULARY A	VOCABULARY B	SPELLING A	SPELLING B	GRAMMAR A	GRAMMAR B	SENTENCE CONSTRUCTION/PUNCTUATION A	SENTENCE CONSTRUCTION/PUNCTUATION B	WRITING A	WRITING B	HOMEWORK
A Home for Grandfather	F	U1														
Homes Around the World	NF	U1													■	
Hansel and Gretel	F	U2														
The Grimm Brothers	NF	U2														
The Mice Who Lived in a Shoe	F	U3														
Rabbits	NF	U3														
'Winter Morning' and 'Snow'	F	U4														
A Contents Page	NF	U4													■	
Animal Tales	F	U5														
A Day at the Zoo	NF	U5														
Merlin	F	U6														
The Vanishing Key Trick	NF	U6														
Theseus and the Minotaur	F	U7														
The Maze Game	NF	U7														
A Poem About Hands	F	U8														
Dirty Hands	NF	U8														
The Mad Hatter's Tea Party	F	U9														
A Birthday Party	NF	U9														
The Cyclone	F	U10														
Hurricane!	NF	U10													■	
Book Reviews	F	U11														
Finding a Book	NF	U11														
I'd Like to be a Teabag	F	U12														
All About Tea	NF	U12														
Check-up	F															
Check-up	NF															

Published by Thomas Nelsor and Sons Ltd

Nelson English © John Jackman and Wendy Wren 2000